Origami

New Ideas for Paperfolding
Origami

Gay Merrill Gross

Principal Photographer Ellen Silverman

Original Diagrams by Gay Merrill Gross   *Illustrations by Anne L. Meskey*

A FRIEDMAN GROUP BOOK

Copyright © 1990 by Michael Friedman Publishing Group, Inc.

ISBN-0-88665-614-1

ORIGAMI: *New Ideas for Paperfolding*
was prepared and produced by
Michael Friedman Publishing Group, Inc.
15 West 26th Street
New York, New York 10010
for WH SMITH LTD.
113 Merton Street
Toronto, Ontario
M4S 1A8

Editor: Sharyn Rosart
Designer: Marcena J. Mulford
Photography Editor: Christopher Bain
Production: Karen L. Greenberg
Illustrator: Anne L. Meskey
Original Diagrams: Gay Merrill Gross
Project Photography © Ellen Silverman
Silhouette Photography © Christopher Bain

Typeset by: Mar + x Myles Graphics
Color separations by Kwong Ming Graphicprint Co.
Printed and bound in Hong Kong by Leefung-Asco Printers Ltd.

Acknowledgments

As a child, I had very few friends as enthusiastic about origami as I was, so I folded alone. It was not until I was an adult that I discovered the pleasure of folding together with other people. The person most responsible for bringing together American paperfolders is Lillian Oppenheimer of New York City, founder of The Origami Center of America in 1958. Her sharing spirit and enthusiasm for origami is the basis for the founding of The Friends of the Origami Center of America in 1980. I now know many extraordinary and wonderful people who are as taken with origami as I am. It is from their generous sharing of their original creations, their techniques and their encouragement that this book is possible.

In particular, I would like to thank:

The creators of the models diagrammed in this book: Joan Appel, Ranana Benjamin, Rae Cooker, John Cunliffe, Alice Gray, Laura Kruskal, Frances LeVangia, Aldo Putignano, Mitsunobu Sonobe, E.D. Sullivan, and Florence Temko.

Alice Gray and Michael Shall for their support and encouragement with this project.

For their ideas used in creating and improving new models, David Shall, Vicente Palacios, Ann Davenport (Purse); Verdi Adams (Envelope); Ranana Benjamin; Joshua Koppel (Howling Dog).

For sharing their ideas and expertise in special techniques, Mark Kennedy, Nate Segal, David Shall, and Katie Kehrig (Paper Painting); Don Sigal (Photocopier Designs); deg farrelly (Paper Bonding); Mark Kennedy and Becky Berman (Protective Coatings); Ros Joyce and Mark Kennedy (Wet Folding); Alice Gray and Michael Shall (Gluing Tips); Alice Gray, Mark Kennedy, and Jean Baden-Gillette (Origami Jewelry); Kathleen O'Regan (Map Folding).

For sharing models used in this book, Dorothy Kaplan (Tulip); Steve and Megumi Biddle (Buttonhole Flower); Tony Cheng and Lillian Oppenheimer for permission to include Inside-Outside Ornament; Shirley Johannesma (Paper Fastener).

For ideas for arrangement of flower models, Idan Schwartz (Tulip); Sara Goldhaber (Buttonhole Flower).

For sample models used in photographs, Aldo Putignano (Bowls).

For many of the papers used in this book, Kate's Paperie (NYC); New York Central Art Supply (NYC).

For Japanese translation, Kyoko Kondo.

For information on paper resources, Carole Restall, Jan Polish, and Mark Kennedy.

For testing diagrams and reviewing text, Alice Gray, Rosalyn Gross, Jan Polish, Mark Kennedy, Michael Shall, and Scott Bedrick.

And Lillian Oppenheimer, a joy to know, and without whom I probably would never have met any of the other people mentioned here.

While some people love to fold paper, others are equally enthusiastic in their appreciation. I gratefully acknowledge the appreciation and support received for so many years from my mother and father as I sat for many hours exploring the possibilities of a folded sheet of paper.

TABLE OF CONTENTS

The origami projects featured in this book are rated according to their level of difficulty. The following symbols appear with each project:

Very easy ◈

Easy ◈ ◈

Intermediate ◈ ◈ ◈

Advanced ◈ ◈ ◈ ◈

Introduction

The pleasures of paperfolding are enjoyed today around the world. Indeed, many different cultures have their own traditions of paperfolding that have contributed to what has become an international art. The strongest tradition, however, comes from Japan, where paperfolding has been practiced for centuries. In recognition of this contribution, many countries have adopted the Japanese word *origami* and use it synonymously with paperfolding. In Japanese, *origami* is a compound word. *Ori* means folded and *kami* means paper. When the two words are combined, the *k* in *kami* becomes a *g*, giving us *origami*.

While the challenge and delight one feels in completing an origami model can be reason enough to fold paper, when the finished model can then be used for some useful or playful purpose, there is a double satisfaction. The origami models in this book were especially selected because they can be used as containers, stationery, gifts, toys, jewelry, or for some other practical purpose.

If you are a beginner to origami, be sure to read carefully through the explanation of symbols and basic folds and refer back to that section as you are following the directions for a particular model. If you are not sure what a particular direction is telling you to do, look ahead to the next drawing—it will show you the end result of the previous step. Try to fold as neatly and as accurately as you can to achieve the best finished results. Following origami diagrams is a little like solving a puzzle or going on a treasure hunt. The hunt is enjoyable in itself, and each direction or clue successfully completed leads you to the final treasure—your finished model.

If you take a finished origami model or even a crumpled piece of paper and unfold it, you will still have your original square with the addition of many crease lines. If you look carefully at these creases, you will see that some bend down like a valley, while some bend up, like a mountain. It is this pattern of valley and mountain creases that when folded in a certain sequence, yields some recognizable form. While following the directions in this book will give you some very nice examples of other peoples' designs, you need not limit your folding to these already-discovered crease patterns. Experiment with models in this book to see what variations you can discover, or just take a piece of paper in your hands and fold it randomly (a paper doodle) and see what develops.

Wishing you much success and enjoyment as you discover the magic of a folded sheet of paper.

—G.M.G.

Part I

INTRODUCTION
TO
ORIGAMI

ORIGAMI SYMBOLS

VALLEY FOLD:
Fold paper forward

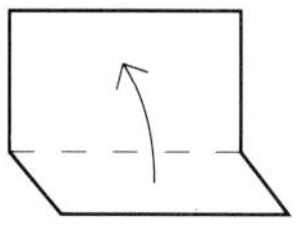

When you open paper that has been valley-folded, you will see a concave crease that bends inward like a groove, or valley. This is called a valley crease.

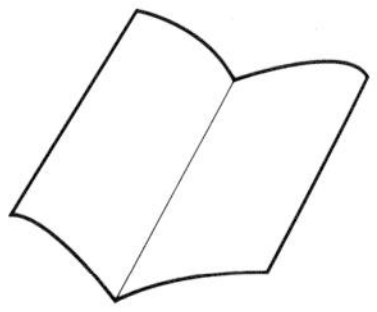

MOUNTAIN FOLD:
Fold paper backward

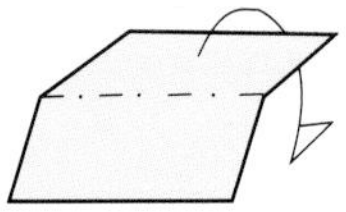

When you open paper that has been mountain-folded, you will see a convex crease that bends outward—it has a little peak you can pinch. This is called a mountain crease.

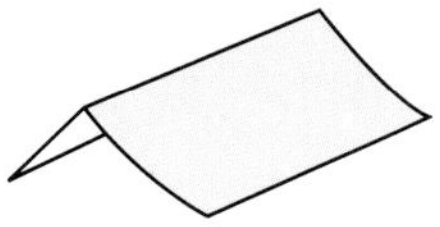

Fold toward you (valley fold) and in direction of arrow.

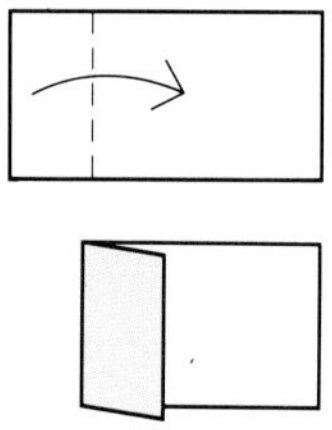

Fold away from you (mountain fold) and in direction of arrow.

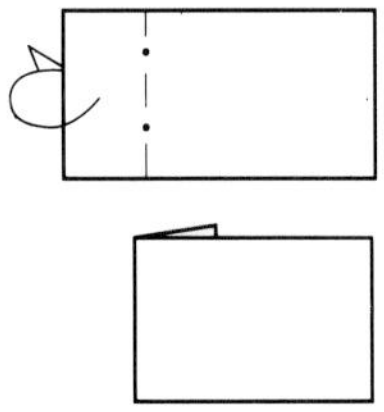

Fold and unfold

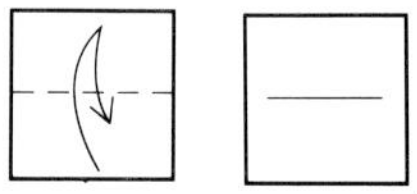

Insert

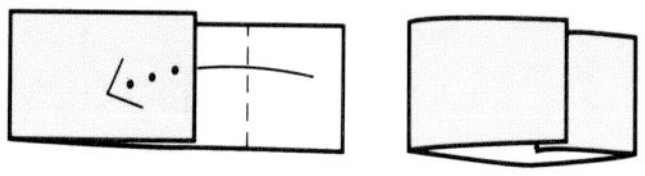

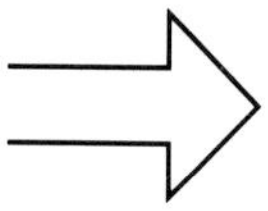

Unfold

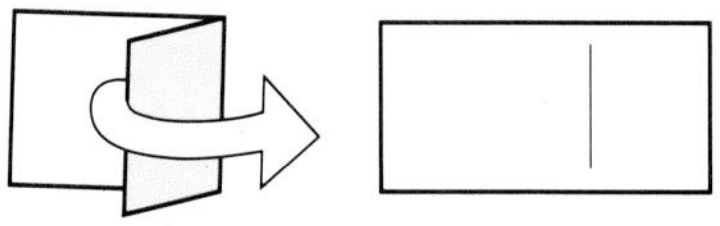

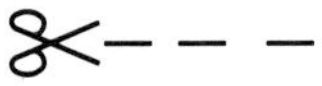

Cut along line

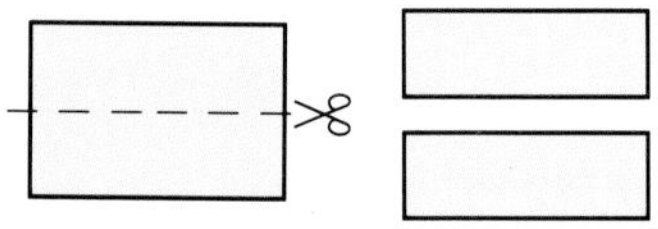

Curve paper (soft crease)

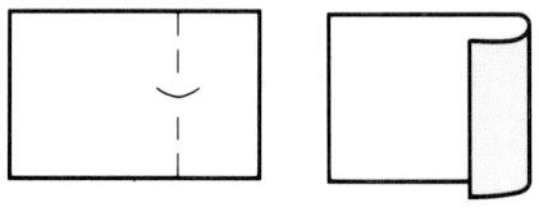

X-ray view

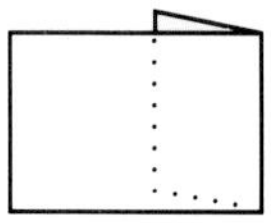

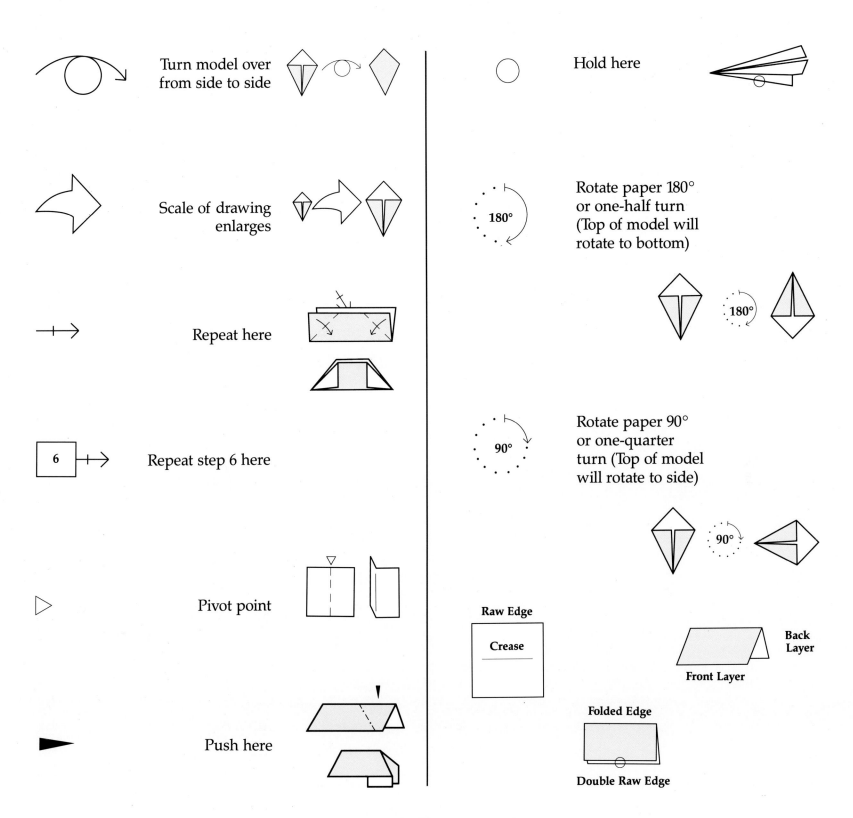

Turn model over from side to side

Scale of drawing enlarges

Repeat here

Repeat step 6 here

6

Pivot point

Push here

Hold here

Rotate paper 180° or one-half turn (Top of model will rotate to bottom)

180°

Rotate paper 90° or one-quarter turn (Top of model will rotate to side)

90°

Raw Edge

Crease

Folded Edge

Double Raw Edge

Front Layer

Back Layer

BASIC FOLDS

Folding patterns that are commonly used throughout origami are given easy-to-remember names based on what they look like when the folds are completed.

BOOK FOLD

Fold one side edge over to lie on opposite side edge.

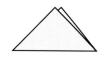

ICE CREAM CONE FOLD

Fold two adjacent sides to meet at center.

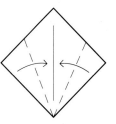 

DIAPER FOLD

Fold one corner to lie over opposite corner.

HOUSE ROOF FOLD

Fold two adjacent corners to meet at center.

CUPBOARD FOLD

Fold two opposite parallel sides towards each other to meet at center.

BLINTZ FOLD

Fold all four corners to meet at center.

Note: Although less easily recognizable, the crease pattern for a sideways ice cream cone fold is still called an "ice cream cone fold." The same is true for all the basic folds.

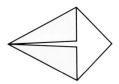

Still an ice cream cone fold.   **Still a book fold.**   **Still a cupboard fold.**

REVERSE FOLDS

In order for you to perform a reverse fold, your model or portion of your model should have a front layer, a back layer, and a folded edge or spine connecting the two layers. In a reverse fold, an end of this double layer of paper is turned either into itself (inside reverse fold) or around itself (outside reverse fold).

INSIDE REVERSE FOLD

1. You may wish to prepare your paper first by performing a simple valley fold that will serve as a precrease.

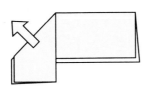

2. Check to be sure this is the shape you would like the paper to ultimately take, then unfold.

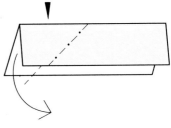

3. Spread the layers of your paper apart. Apply pressure (push in) at the mountain-folded edge (spine) until it changes to a valley fold. At the same time, the pre-creases you made earlier will both become mountain-folded edges.

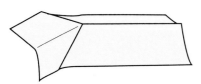

4. This shows the inside reverse fold in progress. Keep applying pressure to end of paper until model can be flattened.

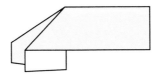

5. One end of your double layer is now "sandwiched" between the front and back layers.

OUTSIDE REVERSE FOLD

Again starting with front and back layers connected by a "spine," you can "wrap" one end around both layers, as if turning a hood onto your head.

1. Mark the place where you want the fold to be (precrease). Unfold.

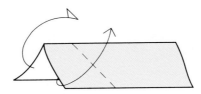

2. Spread layers apart and wrap end around outside of model.

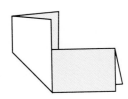

3. Press flat.

FOLDING HINTS

· It is usually easier to fold paper on a hard surface such as a table.

· Fold as neatly and as accurately as you can.

· If the paper you are using is colored or patterned on one side only: Origami directions usually specify which side should be facing up when you begin folding. If this is not indicated, it is usually safe to begin with the white side of the paper facing you.

· It is usually easier to fold paper by bringing an edge from the lower part of the paper up. If you find it easier to fold this way and directions indicate a side-to-side or downward fold, you can always rotate your paper so that the direction of the fold is now upward, and then fold. After folding, reposition your paper so that it looks like the next step in the diagram.

· It is usually easier to make a valley fold in your model than to make a mountain fold. A valley fold becomes a mountain fold when you turn your paper over, so if a diagram indicates to make a mountain fold, you may choose to turn the paper over and make a valley fold. When you turn your paper back to the right side, you will have the desired mountain fold.

· Origami diagrams are usually drawn as if the paper were held loosely rather than pressed flat. This slightly three-dimensional representation is used to give you information about the different layers of paper. If you see a slight gap between edges in a diagram, this would disappear if model were pressed flat.

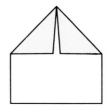
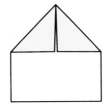

Drawing depicts paper held loosely.   **Your paper should not show gap.**

In general, your paper should be folded right to an edge or crease, *without* leaving a gap, unless otherwise indicated in the written instructions.

ORIGAMI BASES

A combination of folding patterns that gives you a specific form is called an origami base. Most origami models use one of these bases as a starting point.

Most people are familiar with the principle of pleating paper—alternating mountain and valley folds in parallel lines. The two most commonly used origami bases, the preliminary base and the waterbomb base, use the same principle of alternating mountain and valley folds, but this time all the folds intersect at a center point.

DIAMOND BASE

Begin with white side up.

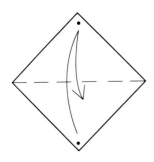

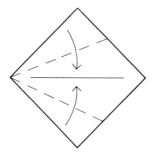

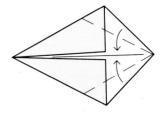

1. Lay square on table so one corner is near you. Bring that corner up to top corner. Crease and unfold.

2. Ice cream cone fold: Bring two raw edges that join at left-side corner together to lie on horizontal center line.

3. Bring raw edges that join at right corner to horizontal center line.

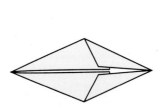

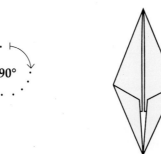

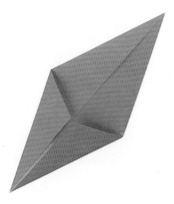

4. Rotate model 90° clockwise so that right corner is now at bottom of model.

5. Completed diamond base.

PRELIMINARY BASE

Begin with a square, white side facing up.

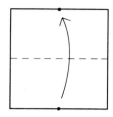

Book fold:

1. Bring bottom raw edge up to meet top raw edge. When edges and corners meet exactly, run your hand along folded edge to form a sharp crease. The fold you have just made is called a book fold.

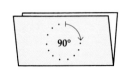

2. Rotate your paper 90° so the folded edge is now vertical . . .

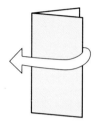

3. . . . unfold—open the book.

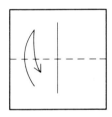

4. Book fold and unfold: You should have a crease marking the vertical center line of your square. Bring the raw edge now at the bottom of your square up to meet the top raw edge. Crease and unfold.

5. You should now have two intersecting valley folds on the white side of your paper. These two creases should look like a plus sign.

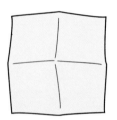

6. Turn your paper over to the colored side. The two creases you just looked at should now appear as mountain folds. Position your paper so it appears diamond-shaped. One corner of the square will be nearest to you.

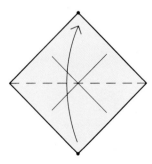

7. Diaper fold: Bring bottom corner up to meet the corner at the top of the diamond. When both corners are precisely aligned, run your hand along the folded edge and make a sharp crease. Your paper should now have the form of a triangle.

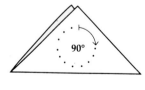

8. Rotate your triangle 90° so the folded edge that was at the base is now at the side.

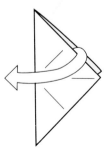

9. Open the triangle.

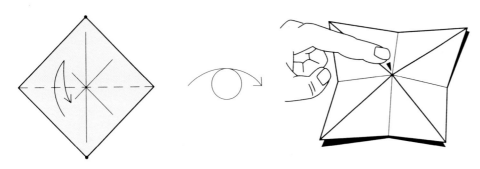

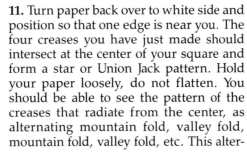

10. Diaper fold and unfold: You should have a valley fold connecting the top and bottom corners of your diamond shape. We will now make a crease connecting the two side corners of the diamond. Bring the bottom corner up to meet the top corner and crease at the base of the triangle. Unfold your paper.

11. Turn paper back over to white side and position so that one edge is near you. The four creases you have just made should intersect at the center of your square and form a star or Union Jack pattern. Hold your paper loosely, do not flatten. You should be able to see the pattern of the creases that radiate from the center, as alternating mountain fold, valley fold, mountain fold, valley fold, etc. This alter-

nating crease pattern should give your paper a spring, or tension. Place your finger in very center of square (where all creases intersect), and push center point up and down. As you pop in one direction, the four corners of square should pop in opposite direction. Leave center pushed down, and four corners should be pointing up.

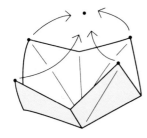

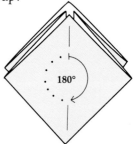

12. Using both hands, push all four corners of square together at same time.

13. Your paper should resemble a flower bud, open on top and closed at the bottom. You should see four flaps extending from the central axis of your model. Flatten the model, bringing two flaps together on each side.

14. Rotate your model so that the closed end is now at the top, and flatten.

15. You should have two flaps at each side of a diamond-shaped square. This is called a preliminary base because it is the basis for making a great many origami models.

WATERBOMB BASE

The waterbomb base is named after a traditional model called the Waterbomb or Paper Balloon, which starts from this base.

Note: The preliminary base and waterbomb base are made from the same creasing pattern; one is the other turned inside out.

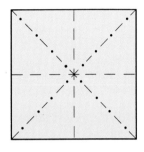

1. Begin as for preliminary base, only start with colored side of paper up.

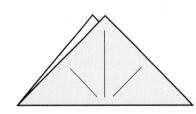

2. Continue through step 10 of preliminary base but leave last diaper fold in place. Rotate paper so that point will be at bottom.

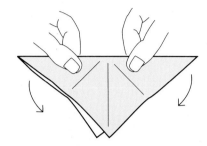

3. This step must be done holding the paper in the air. Lift up diaper fold so that the folded edge is at the top and hold this edge with both hands. As you push your hands together, the near layer of your paper will pop forward, and the far layer will push back.

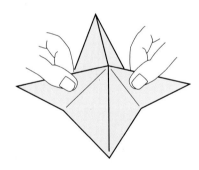

4. (View from top.) You should see four points projecting from the central axis of your model, like a star. Continue to push your hands together as far as you can.

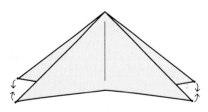

5. Flatten your model so that two flaps rest at each side.

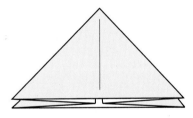

6. Finished waterbomb base. The surface of your model is the shape of a triangle, but if you look under the bottom edge, you will see additional layers of paper.

UMBRELLA BASE

Begin with a preliminary base. Drawing shows side view of preliminary base and inside layers.

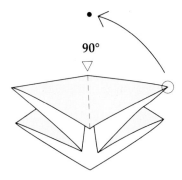

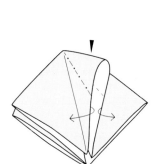

Squash fold:

1. Begin to lift up one side flap of your preliminary base as if you were turning the page in a book, but stop when the flap is standing straight up in the air at a right angle to the rest of your model.

2. Notice that this flap takes the shape of a triangle. One sloping side is a folded edge and one sloping side is a double raw edge that can be opened. As you separate the two raw edges, push down on the folded edge so that it unfolds. What was a triangular flap standing up has now been flat-

tened or squashed into a tall triangle with two small triangle "feet." Down the middle of the tall triangle is a mountain crease where the folded edge had been; make sure this crease runs down the center of your model and connects with the gap you see between the two triangle "feet."

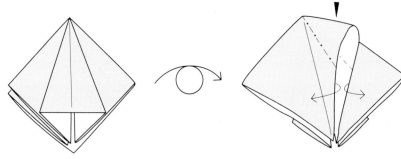

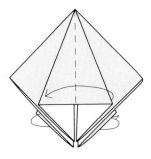

3. When everything is lined up and centered, run your fingers along the sides of the tall triangle and press flat. The move you have just done is called a squash fold.

4. Turn your model over and repeat from step 1, squashing another of the flaps from your original preliminary base.

5. You will be squashing all four of the original flaps on the preliminary base. You have already squashed two (front and back); now you need to squash the flaps that are protruding at the sides. Each flap you have already squashed created two half-size flaps. Turn the right half-size flap over to meet the left one as if turning the page of a book. For accurate folding it is important to keep your model balanced (same number of flaps on each side of the central axis). At this point, turn your model over and repeat this step on the back.

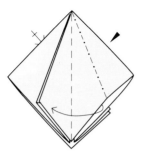
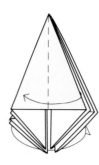
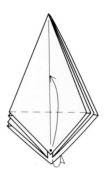

6. On the right you will now have exposed another full-size flap to squash. Repeat steps 1 through 3 on this flap. Turn over and repeat on back.

7. You should now have eight half-size flaps in total. Be sure your model is balanced—four flaps on each side. Bring the top right flap over to the left (turn the page). Turn your model over and repeat behind.

8. The surface you have just exposed is a solid shape (upside-down kite) with a smooth surface. Lift the bottom point up, front layer only, as far as it will go. Repeat behind.

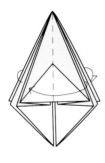

9. Your tall triangle will now have a smaller triangle sitting at its base. Fold first two flaps on right over to left (turn two pages). Repeat behind.

10. Repeat step 8, front and back.

11. Unfold your model completely. Lay it on table with white side up.

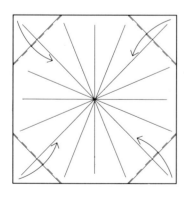
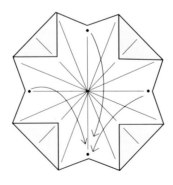
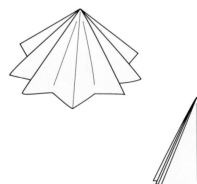

12. At each corner of your square is a triangular shape with a mountain fold at its base. Change this mountain to a valley fold, so that the outside corner and a small colored triangle are turned in and rest on white side of paper. Turn in all four corners of square.

13. Your paper is now shaped like an octagon. Using the creases already in your paper, re-form it into the tall triangular shape you had before you opened your paper, only now you no longer have a small white triangle showing.

14. When held loosely, it should resemble an umbrella.

15. Flatten your model and make sure it is balanced—four flaps on each side. This is your umbrella base.

BIRD BASE

Begin with preliminary base. Place on table so that closed point is away from you and opening is near you.

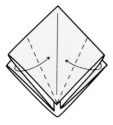

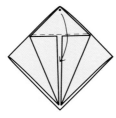

1. You should have two flaps (a front and a back flap) on each side of the preliminary base. Bring the double raw edges from one front flap over to sit on the center line. Repeat on the other front flap.

2. You have made an ice cream cone fold with the front layers of your model. Fold top triangle ("ice cream") down, using top of "cone" as your guide.

3. Leaving triangular flap folded down, unfold ice cream cone creases made in step 1.

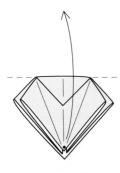

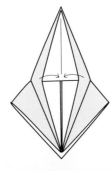

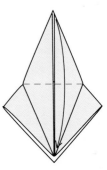

4. There are several layers of paper exposed at bottom of model. Lift up bottom point of front layer only. Swing point all the way up as far as you can—the fold you made when you turned down the "ice cream" will be your guide. (Triangular flap will also swing up.)

5. The front of your model will look like a boat. Bring the long side edges of the boat (raw edges) together so they meet each other and sit on the vertical center line. Make sure the top and bottom points are even. Run your finger around the folded edges to sharpen.

6. Bring the top point down to the bottom of the model.

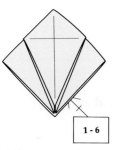

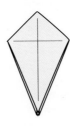

7. Turn model over and repeat steps 1 through 6 on the back.

8. This is your completed bird base. It is so called because the traditional Japanese Crane and Flapping Bird as well as many

other bird models can be folded from this base. It is the starting point for many other models as well.

Part II

PAPERFOLDING
PROJECTS

HOPPING BUNNY
by Gay Merrill Gross
(based on the traditional Jumping Frog)

❖ ❖

Paper: In order to "hop," this model must be folded from stiff paper or a lightweight card such as a business card or a small file card.
You will need a rectangle; the smaller the size, the better the bunny will hop. A 3″ x 5″ (7 x 13 cm) file card will work, a 2″ x 3½″ (5 x 9 cm) business card will work even better.

Writing side up

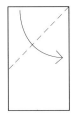

1. Bring top edge down at an angle to lie over right-side edge.

2. Crease very hard at folded edge, then unfold.

3. Bring top edge down to lie over left-side edge. Crease hard and unfold.

4. The two creases you have made form an X at top of rectangle. These creases are valley folds because they bend in like a valley.

Turn card over. You should still have an X at top of card, but creases are now mountain folds because each crease resembles a mountain peak and can be pinched.

5. Bring top edge of card down so top corners touch bottom of X— you are folding right through the center of the X.

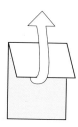

6. Unfold.

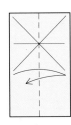 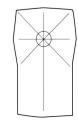

7. Bring long edges of card together in a book fold. Crease and unfold.

Turn card over. (Back to side with writing.)

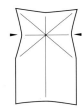

8. Push finger in at circle—where all creases intersect. Top corners of card will pop up as intersection point pops down.

9. Push in at both sides, where horizontal mountain creases meet outside edges.

10. Bring top edge down over card and two inner layers.

11. You now have a triangular shape sitting on top of your card. Swing right point of triangle over to left.

12. Bring right-side edge over to lie along center crease. Crease very, very hard.

13. Swing both free points over to left.

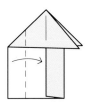

14. Bring left-side edge over to lie along center crease.

15. Swing top point back to left side.

16. Model looks like an arrow pointing up. Turn over.

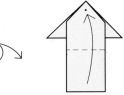

17. Bring bottom edge up to slightly below top point.
Drawing gets larger.

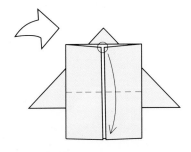

18. Bring double raw edge down to bottom folded edge.

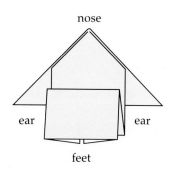

nose

ear   ear

feet

19. Model looks like this.

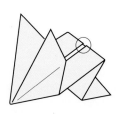

20. Place model on table as shown—nose and feet rest on table. Lift ears up.

With one finger at circle, press down folded edge behind ears to table, slide finger off model with a snap, and bunny will hop!

HOWLING DOG
by Gay Merrill Gross

◆ ◆ ◆ ◆

Paper: Make from a square, approximately 6″ to 9″ (15 to 23 cm).

Note: This model contains several reverse folds. Be sure you are familiar with this procedure before beginning the model.

1. Begin with diamond base. Fold bottom point up at place where obtuse corners meet on center line.

2. Smaller triangle will become tail. Narrow tail by bringing sides of this triangle to meet at center line. At same time you will need to accommodate base of triangle by squashing to make two irregularly shaped small triangles (see next drawing).

3. Lift tail and fold down at point where two bottom triangles meet.

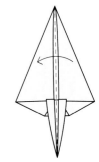

4. Book-fold body and tail in half.

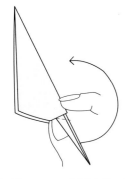

5. Outside-reverse-fold tail—slip thumb into groove of tail. As you reverse tail inside out, swing it to the side and up.

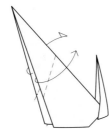

6. Outside-reverse-fold top point.

7. Outside-reverse-fold to form head.

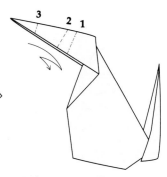

8. To form snout: First precrease folds at end of point to desired shape (see next drawing), then unfold and form reverse folds in order shown.

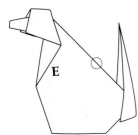

9. To make dog howl: Hold dog at circle with one hand. With other hand push folded edge E (front and back) toward head end of dog.

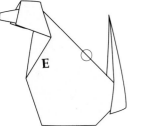

10. Howling Dog.

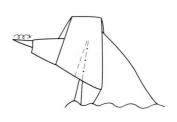

Optional
Nose: Reverse-fold point out to front of snout. Roll up tip of point and pull up to rest at top of snout.

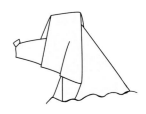

Ear: Crimp to suggest ear.

KISSING PENGUINS

by E. D. Sullivan

◆ ◆ ◆

**Paper: Origami paper, black on one side, white on reverse side.
You will need a 6″ (15 cm) square.**

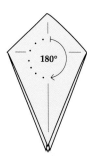

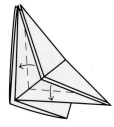

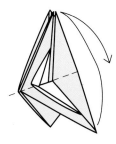

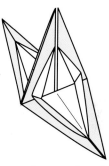

1. Begin with a black bird base. Rotate your bird base 180° so that the closed point is now at the bottom.

2. Bring top front point (wing flap) down until it stands straight up at a right angle to rest of model.

3. Lift one raw edge from center of model and pull away from center, exposing the white side of that layer. Crease along lines shown.

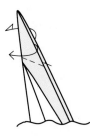

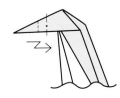

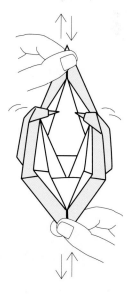

4. Reclose the wing flap to set the creases in the reverse fold you have made. When you open the wing down again, you will see that you have formed the white breast on the front of one penguin.

5. Repeat from step 3, on the other side and on back, trying to keep amount reverse-folded out approximately equal on all sides.

6. The two points at the top of model will form the penguins' heads.

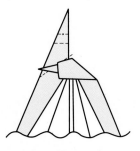

7. Outside-reverse-fold one point as shown.

8. Reach inside head and pleat as shown to form beak.

9. Repeat steps 7 and 8 on other point to form head and beak on that side.

10. Pull wing flaps in and out, and penguin heads will touch as if kissing. If beaks do not meet, adjust angle of heads slightly until they do.

TULIP
(Traditional)

◆ ◆ ◆

**Paper: Colorful origami paper or wrapping paper. You'll
need a square approximately 4″ to 6″ (10 to 15 cm).**

Begin with a colored waterbomb base.

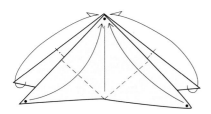

1. On front layer, fold right and left bottom
points up to top point. Turn over and repeat on
back of model.

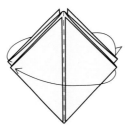

2. Turn pages: Fold right-side point (front point
only) over to left side. Turn over and repeat
behind.

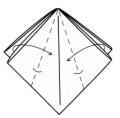

3. Beginning fold at top point, bend right and
left front flaps toward each other to form a
loose upside-down ice cream cone shape, but
do not crease yet.

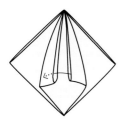

4. Slip one double-folded edge inside the other.
Push together till you get a tight fit, then flatten
the model so that . . .

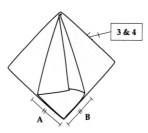

3 & 4

A   B

5. . . . distance A equals distance B. Repeat
steps 3 and 4 on back of model.

6. At bottom of model, separate front and back
layers and blow into hole at bottom to inflate
flower. Flatten base of flower.

7. One at a time, curl each of the four slender
points at top of flower outward and "peel"
down halfway to form petal.

8. Finished Tulip. Insert stem end of Standing
Leaf and Stem (see page 34) into hole at bottom
of flower.

STANDING LEAF AND STEM
by Mitsunobu Sonobe

Paper: Origami or any other paper in a shade of green. You'll need a square approximately 6" (15 cm). If you are using Standing Leaf and Stem with Tulip, Leaf and Stem can be folded from square that is same size or slightly larger than square used for Tulip.

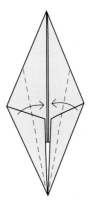

1. Begin with diamond base. Narrow bottom.

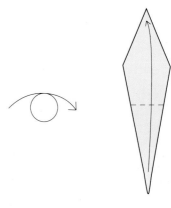

2. Turn model over from side to side (narrowed point remains at bottom).

3. Fold bottom point up to top point.

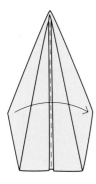

4. Book-fold in half.

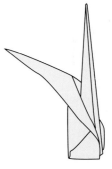

5. Outside-reverse-fold outer point to form leaf. Crease softly.

6. If balanced correctly, Leaf and Stem will stand. Poke stem end into a flower with a hole at base such as the Tulip.

BUTTONHOLE FLOWER
by Mitsunobu Sonobe

❖ ❖ ❖ ❖

Paper: Origami paper or colored notepaper. You'll need a square 3" to 6" (7 to 15 cm). Follow instructions for the umbrella base through step 10, reversing all color instructions so that the inside of the model will be colored. When the flower is opened, the color will show.

Hold model with narrow point at bottom.

View from side.

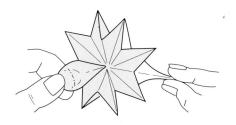

1. Precrease: Make diagonal valley folds starting at colored point. (You are folding through all layers of paper.) Then pinch narrow point in half with a mountain fold.

2. At the top of the flower you have eight flaps, which will become petals. Pull the two outermost flaps toward each other until they meet and the rest of the petals spread apart as flower opens.

3. Insert thumb into one petal, and give it a round shape by flattening the outer slanted folded edge between thumb and index finger. To set this shape and keep petal open, push up slightly with forefinger, creating a small mountain crease. Repeat on all petals.

4. Buttonhole Flower in full bloom. Insert stem end into the pocket of the Buttonhole Leaf and Stem or the Cactus Plant (see pages 36 and 37).

BUTTONHOLE LEAF AND STEM
Variation of model by Alice Gray

**Paper: Origami paper or similar paper in a shade of green.
Use the same size square you used to fold the flower.**

Begin with a diamond base. Hold it so that the sides folded to center last are at the bottom of model.

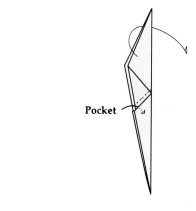

Pocket

1. Wide V formed by folded edges points to stem end. Book-fold model in half.

2. Narrow stem end of front layer. Turn over and repeat behind.

3. Find lower pocket and mountain-fold leaf end back, creating a crease that is slightly above and parallel to the folded edge of pocket.

4. To shape leaf: Push down at mountain fold near end of leaf, slightly curling up tip of leaf.

5. Insert stem end of flower into pocket.

6. Mountain-pinch pocket area in half. This will narrow stem and help to hold flower securely. For added security, place glue on stem end of the flower before inserting into pocket in step 5.

CACTUS PLANT

Variation on models by Mitsunobu Sonobe, Rae Cooker, and Florence Temko

❖ ❖ ❖

Paper: Origami or wrapping paper in a shade of green.
You'll need a square approximately 6″ to 8″ (15 to 20 cm)

Fold Teardrop Ornament (see page 58) up to step 5.

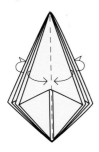

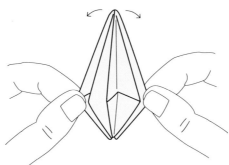

1. Separate all eight side flaps so that they are equidistant from one another.

2. Hold two opposite flaps between thumb and forefinger of each hand. As you slowly pull your hands apart, the top point will begin to spread apart and flatten. As soon as the tip is slightly flattened, move your hands to hold two different opposite flaps and spread the tip out a little further. Continue rotating the flaps you tug at as you spread the top of the model until it loses its point and is rounded to your liking.

3. Finished Cactus.

Insert tiny Buttonhole Flower into one pocket of plant and let the cactus rest on a Flowerpot (see page 38).

FLOWERPOT
by Florence Temko

◆ ◆ ◆

Paper: Most varieties of paper will work well with this model. Almost any size square, 6″ (15 cm) and larger, can be used. Note—use same size paper you use for Cactus Plant.

*A variation on this model is also part of the Spanish tradition of paperfolding.

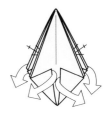

1. Begin with umbrella base. Your umbrella base has eight flaps and eight side corners, one at the outside of each flap. Make sure your model is balanced—four flaps on each side. Bring the side corner of both front flaps up so that bottom edges meet at center line. Turn over and repeat behind.

2. Swing front-side point at right over to left. Turn over and repeat behind.

3. On front layer, bring right- and left-side points up to center. Turn over and repeat behind.

4. All eight side points have now been folded up. Unfold all eight points (two on front, two on back, and four on inside layers).

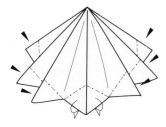

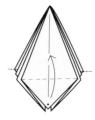

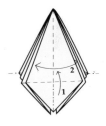

5. Loosely open out the bottom of the umbrella base and spread flaps apart. On existing creases, reverse-fold one side point inside model. Repeat on the other seven points.

6. Flatten model in a balanced position—four flaps on each side. On the front layer, lift the bottom point up as far as you can. Turn over and repeat behind.

7. Lift front right-side flap and fold over to left (turn one page of book). Turn over and repeat behind.

8. Repeat steps 6 and 7 until all the bottom points have been turned up. (Remember to always keep the model balanced—same number of flaps on each side.)

180°

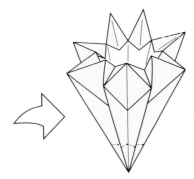

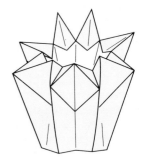

9. Fold the top point down to touch the top of the small triangle.* Crease hard and unfold.

*This crease determines the height of the Flowerpot. If you would like a shallower pot, fold the point farther down.

Rotate model 180°.

10. To open Flowerpot: Spread the side flaps as wide apart as possible. Insert a finger of one hand into the opening. With the

other hand push the bottom point up. By pinching between two fingers, reinforce as mountain folds the creases that outline the base of the pot.

11. Finished Flowerpot. When using the Flowerpot to hold origami flowers, you may want to weigh down the bottom by adding pennies or sand.

BOWL
by Aldo Putignano

◆ ◆ ◆

Paper: Wallpaper, a colorful shopping bag, or foil paper. You'll need a square approximately 10″ to 18″ (26 to 45 cm). Start with the white side up.

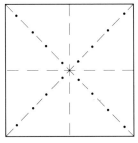

1. Put in creases to make a preliminary base by following steps 1 to 10. Do not close up into preliminary base; leave the paper open, white side facing up.

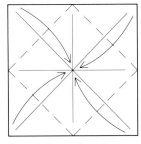

2. Blintz fold: Fold each corner to center of square.

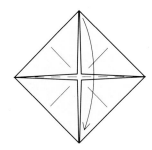

3. Fold top point down to bottom point.

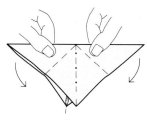

4. Using both hands, hold model at top edge. Push hands together and form model into a waterbomb base with two flaps on each side. (This is called a blintzed waterbomb base because the blintz fold you made in step 2 adds an extra layer inside your model.)

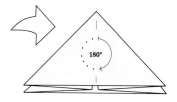

5. Rotate your model so that top point is now at bottom of model.

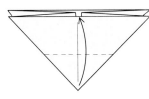

6. Fold bottom point up to center of top edge.

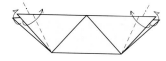

7. Front layer only, fold slanted folded edges toward center—crease should originate where slanted side edge meets bottom folded edge. Repeat behind.

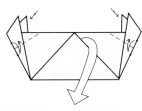

8. Unfold bottom fold. You now have four tabs protruding up. Fold both front tabs down at an angle so that folded edge lies along itself. Crease and unfold. Turn over and repeat behind.

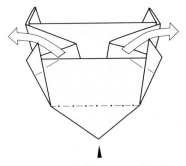

9. Open model from top, leaving protruding tabs in place. Flatten model at bottom using existing creases as your guide.

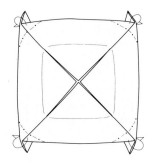

10. (View inside model.) At each corner, mountain-fold point back, using existing creases.

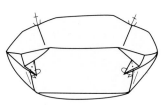

11. (View from side of model.) At each corner of the bowl, mountain-fold point back and tuck into pocket behind it.

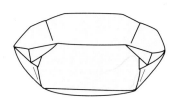

12. Finished Bowl.

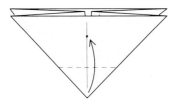

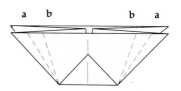

To make a deeper bowl:
At step 6, fold bottom point up so that it lies on the center line, but below the top edge. The lower you bring the point, the deeper your bowl will be. Bear in mind that the shorter the length of the new folded edge at the bottom, the less of a base your bowl will have to sit on. The sides of the bowl can also be varied by changing the angle at which you fold the sides in at step 7. The nearer to the center you bring the side points, the steeper the sides of the bowl will be. After you have folded up one side, use it as a guide to make sure the other corners are folded in at the same angle.

Choose angle a or angle b, or anywhere in between.

HEART VALENTINE CARD
by Gay Merrill Gross
(adapted from model by Joan Appel)

◆ ◆ ◆

Paper: Paper or foil, red or pink on one side, white on the reverse side. You'll need a 2:1 rectangle. The finished model will be one-half the width of the original sheet. (e.g., a 12" x 6" (30 x 15 cm) rectangle will make a card 3" (7.5 cm) square.)

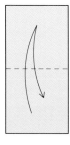

1. Begin with the colored side up. Fold bottom short edge up to top edge. Crease and unfold.

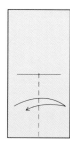

2. Bring long-side edges together, but only crease bottom half of rectangle. Unfold.

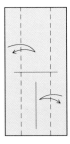

3. Cupboard-fold (long-side edges to center) and unfold.

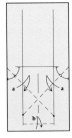

4. a) Make diagonal creases in lower square, but do not crease beyond indicated points (use cupboard-fold creases as a guide).

b) Bring bottom raw edge up to meet same points where diagonal creases end. Crease only between cupboard creases. Unfold.

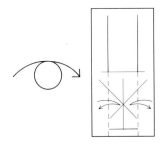

5. Turn paper over to white side. Change cupboard creases in bottom square to valley creases on white side. Crease and unfold.

6. Cupboard-fold top and bottom edges to center. Unfold.

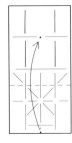

7. Bring bottom edge to horizontal valley crease nearest to top edge.

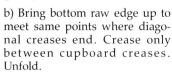
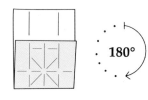

8. Rotate model 180° so that folded edge will be at top.

9. Fold top corners down to nearest intersection of creases. Crease and unfold.

10. On front layer only, bring side raw edges to meet inside model—use mountain cupboard creases already there. At same time, accommodate at top folded edge by pushing in along existing diagonal creases of front layer.

11. Bring bottom corners of colored panel to nearest horizontal crease, then unfold.

12. As you lift front raw edge at bottom of colored panel (on existing crease), push in folded edges at sides of panel to form two small squash folds.

  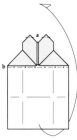 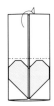

13. Fold up corners.

14. On middle colored panel, push in sides near top using the waterbomb creases already existing. Lower part of middle panel will swing upward.

15. a) Mountain-fold tips back to round off top points of heart.

b) Mountain-fold white section back and upward so that it lies behind heart.

16. Cupboard-fold sides to center, slipping flaps under heart.

17. Fold top edge of model backward to meet bottom edge.

18. Finished Card. Write a message inside to your valentine!

ENVELOPE
by Frances LeVangia

◆ ◆ ◆

Paper: Bond or typing paper in white or colors works well. Higher quality bond paper with a textured finish can make a nice stationery set. You'll need an 8½″ x 11″ (21.5 x 28 cm) or larger rectangle to make an envelope large enough for mailing. If you would like the finished envelope to fit a square card, start with a 2:3 rectangle.

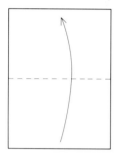

1. Hold paper so that short sides are at top and bottom. Fold bottom edge up to top edge.

2. Fold down top edge of front layer only.

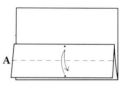

3. Bring bottom raw edge up to folded edge to form crease A. Unfold.

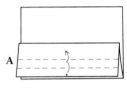

4. Fold bottom raw edge to crease A and then roll up, refolding on crease A.

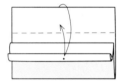

5. Bring top edge down to slightly above folded edge nearest to bottom edge. Unfold.

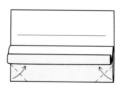

6. Fold bottom corners up to folded edge.

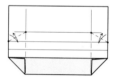

7. Use vertical sides of triangular flaps formed in last step as your guide. Fold side edges of model inward in line with sides of triangles. Crease and unfold.

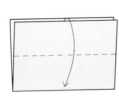

8. Connect the dots: Make a small diagonal valley fold on each side. Fold starts where top folded edge meets side edge and ends at intersection of vertical and horizontal creases. Crease and unfold.

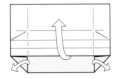

9. Unfold top folded edge and triangular flaps.

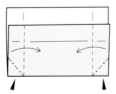

10. Fold side edges of front layer only inward on existing creases. At bottom of model, squash open to triangular shape.

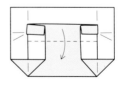

11. Fold flap down on existing crease.

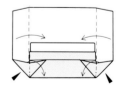

12. Triangles at bottom of model open and then close flat. At same time, sides of model fold inward.

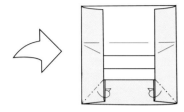

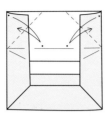

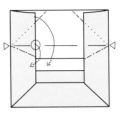

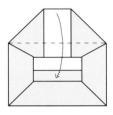

13. At bottom of model, use existing slanting creases to mountain-fold double front layer under itself, locking corners inside model.

14. Bring top corners down so that folded edges at sides lie along horizontal crease nearest to top edge of model. Crease and unfold.

15. With finger at circle, slide vertical raw edge inside envelope, at same time outside folded edge swings down 90°, changing from vertical to horizontal position in line with existing horizontal crease. Repeat on right side.

16. Tuck top edge into pocket.

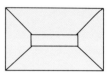

17. Finished Envelope.

To Make Note Cards to Fit Envelope:

Use the same paper you used for the envelope.

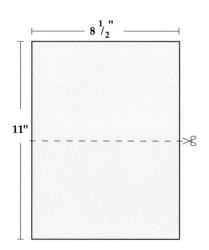

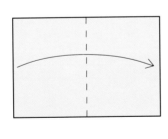

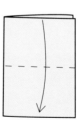

1. Cut sheet in half—each half will make one card.

2. Book-fold in half . . .

3. . . . and in half again.

4. If you wish, decorate the outside of the Card with a small origami model.

PAPER FASTENER

by John Cunliffe

This clever model will securely and attractively hold together several sheets of paper.
Paper: Origami paper or lightweight wrapping paper. You'll need approximately 2″ to 2 ¹/₂″ (5 to 7 cm) square.

1. Fold small square into a waterbomb base. Slip top left corner of loose sheets you wish to "fasten" together into far opening of waterbomb base. Corners of loose sheets should touch top point of waterbomb base.

2. Bring top point of waterbomb base to bottom raw edge. You will be folding through all layers of waterbomb base as well as all layers of the inserted sheets. Crease very hard.

3. Fold loose side points almost to center of base line, being sure to leave a small gap between the double-folded side edges of the center triangle and the folded edges you have just brought in line with it.

4. On either side of the center triangle you now have a small triangular flap. Fold both flaps up as far as you can. The crease you make will run right through the small gap you left between folded edges. Crease and unfold.

5. On one side of center triangle, slightly spread double-folded edges apart to open "pocket." Slip triangular flap into this pocket. Repeat on other side.

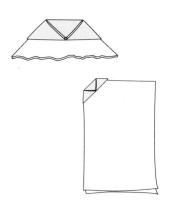

6. Locked Paper Fastener.

Variation: Fold the Fastener at the top right corner of your sheets. When finished, turn the sheets over. The Fastener will be on the left side and the lock will be hidden.

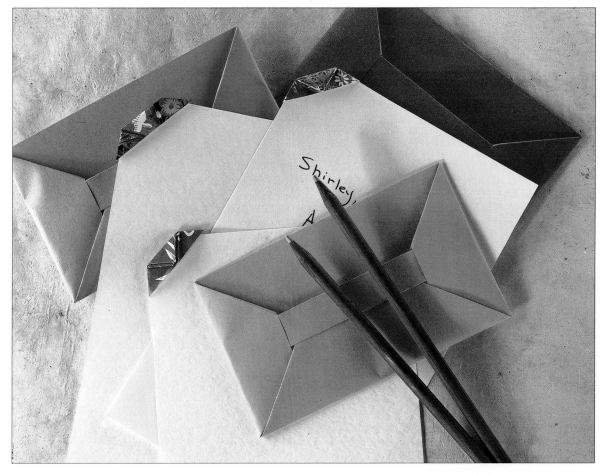

HEART PHOTO FRAME
by Aldo Putignano

❖ ❖

Paper: Use sturdy paper—foil works very well—or laminate tissue or wrapping paper on to foil paper. A 10″ (26 cm) square will make a frame large enough to hold a photo that is 3½″ (9 cm) high x 5″ (12.5 cm) wide.

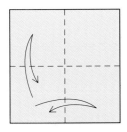

1. Begin with colored side up. Book-fold and unfold in both directions.

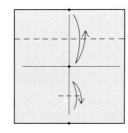

2. Bring top edge to horizontal center line as for cupboard fold. Crease and unfold. Repeat with bottom edge, but only crease (pinch) near center of folded edge. Unfold.

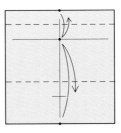

3. Fold top edge to cupboard crease made in step 2. Fold bottom edge to same cupboard crease. Unfold both folds.

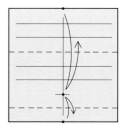

4. Fold bottom edge to pinch. Fold top edge to pinch. Unfold both folds.

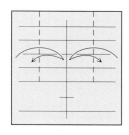

5. Begin to cupboard-fold side edges to center, but only crease from horizontal crease above pinch to top edge (see diagram). Unfold.

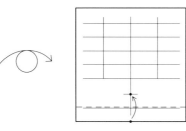

6. Turn over to white side. Fold up on lowermost horizontal crease.

7. Fold bottom corners up to intersection of vertical cupboard creases and horizontal crease that lies above raw edge you just folded up.

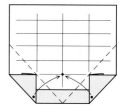

8. Fold new bottom corners up to meet at vertical center line. To ensure neatness, align edges and corners you fold up with underlying "grid" of intersecting creases.

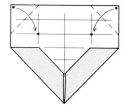

9. Fold top corners down to intersection of cupboard creases and second horizontal crease from top edge.

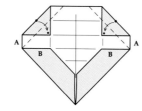

10. You have just folded down two small colored triangles. Bring folded edge of each triangle down to touch opposite corner of that triangle. (Raw edge A will lie next to raw edge B.)

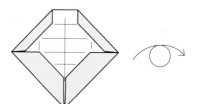

11. Turn model over.

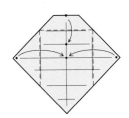

12. Fold top edge down on uppermost horizontal crease. Fold side corners to center (on existing creases).

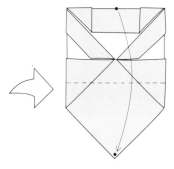 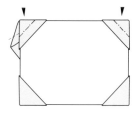 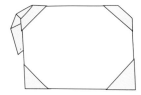 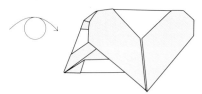

13. Fold top edge down to bottom point.

14. Reverse-fold top corners inside model.

15. Separate front and back layers of model slightly so that Frame will stand. Slip corners of picture or a written message under corners of Frame.

Back layer supports Frame and is shaped like a heart.

PRACTICAL PURSE
by Gay Merrill Gross

◆ ◆ ◆

Paper: Wrapping paper, foil paper, or bond paper. You can create a pattern on bond paper by photocopying a small geometric pattern onto paper. This model is especially attractive when duo paper is used, or two different-colored sheets are folded together. Use a square, any size. Approximately 8½″ (22 cm) square makes a practical-sized purse. The side facing up now will be the color of the inside (lining) of the purse.

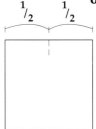

1. Pinch center of top edge.

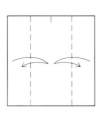

2. Cupboard-fold and unfold: Using pinch mark as a guide, bring left- and right-side edges to meet at center. Open.

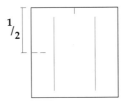

3. Pinch 1/2 mark on one side edge.

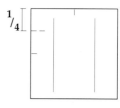

4. Bring top edge to 1/2 mark and pinch side edge, creating 1/4 pinch.

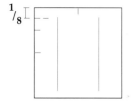

5. Bring top edge to 1/4 mark and pinch side edge, creating 1/8 pinch.

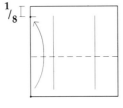

6. Bring bottom edge to 1/8 mark. Crease folded edge all of the way across.

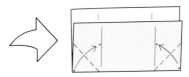

7. Fold up bottom corners so that folded edges lie along the vertical cupboard creases you made in step 2.

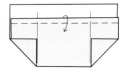

8. On the front layer, fold down horizontal raw edge to create a narrow strip or small hem.

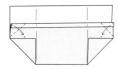

9. Bring corners at end of hem down so that side raw edges of front layer lie along upper edges of triangular flaps—leave a small gap between edges.

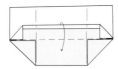

10. Bring folded edge of hem as far down as it will go—you will be creating a fold that runs through the gap between upper and lower triangles.

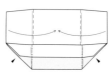

11. Pull upper folded edge of front layer slightly forward to separate front layers from back layer of model. Push inward at slanted folded edges near bottom of model so that they reverse fold inside model. You will also be folding on existing vertical cupboard creases as side raw edges fold in and meet at center.

12. Step 11 in progress.

House-roof-fold:

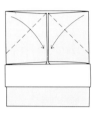

13. Fold top corners down so that each half of the double raw edge at top of model lies along vertical center line.

14. Fold up bottom edges of "roof" to lie along top sloped edges of roof.

15. Slightly unfold last fold and house-roof-fold.

16. On right side, grasp mountain fold that juts out and pull down (front layer only) until you have the form of a large colored triangle with a smaller white triangle protruding out from under the raw edge (see next drawing).

17. Repeat step 16 on left side. As you pull down on the mountain-folded edge, insert protruding small white triangle under raw edge of right side.

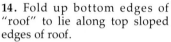

18. Using existing crease, mountain-fold lower triangular area behind itself to lock.

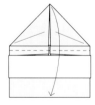

19. Bring top point down to bottom of model.

20. Fold point at bottom of triangular flap backward (mountain fold), and tuck point up into pocket behind it.

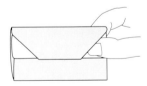

21. Purse is locked. To open, slip finger under top flap and pull up.

22. Open Purse. Use to hold coins, pins, tissues, pills, buttons, sewing kit, business cards, or other items.

WALLET

by Laura Kruskal

◆

Paper: One sheet of computer paper is just the right size—ignore the holes as you fold, they will not show on finished Wallet. For a more decorative Wallet, use wrapping paper, wallpaper, handmade Japanese paper, or marbleized paper. You'll need a 13" x 15" (33 x 38 cm) rectangle.

1. Start with colored side up, and long sides at top and bottom. Book-fold and unfold: Fold bottom edge up to top edge. Crease and unfold. Turn paper over.

2. Cupboard-fold: Fold long sides to meet at horizontal center line. Turn paper over.

3. Book-fold and unfold: Fold left short side over to right side. Crease and unfold.

4. Cupboard-fold and unfold: Fold right and left sides to meet at vertical center line. Crease and unfold.

5. Fold top corners down so that top half of side edges lies along horizontal center line.

6. Refold on cupboard creases made in step 4.

 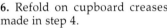

7. At center of bottom edge are two loose corners. Fold each corner up to horizontal center line to create two triangular flaps. Crease and unfold.

8. As you fold bottom edge up to top edge, lock top and bottom halves together by inserting triangular flaps behind slanted folded edges.

9. View inside Wallet. Divider between compartments can be used to separate different denominations of currency.

10. Fold Wallet in half.

11. Finished Wallet. This model makes a great lightweight wallet. Use it every day or when traveling as an extra wallet for foreign currency. It also makes a very nice wrapping when giving money as a gift.

SECRET RING

by Ranana Benjamin

◆ ◆

Paper: Foil paper. You'll need a rectangular strip approximately 1¹/₄" wide x 6¹/₄" long (3.5 x 16 cm). For a larger ring, start with a longer strip.

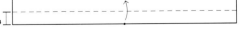

1. Begin with the non-foil side facing up. Fold long bottom edge up 1/3.

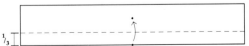

2. Fold top edge down to bottom folded edge, along the raw edge you just folded up.

3. Rotate strip 90° so long edges are at sides.

Drawing gets larger and shows only top end of strip.

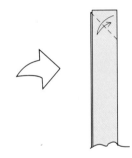

4. Bring top short edge to lie over long edge, make a diagonal crease, and unfold.

5. Using the bottom of your diagonal crease as a guide, fold top short edge down to form a tab that lies directly over rest of strip.

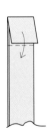

6. Fold down along raw edges.

7. Unfold both horizontal creases, then turn strip over.

8. Swing top of strip diagonally to right so that lower horizontal crease lines up with right long edge.

9. Fold down along horizontal folded edge.

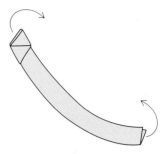

10. Mountain-fold short horizontal strip behind longer vertical strip and swing around to left.

11. Notice the pocket created by the diagonal fold at the top of the long strip. Fold over the short tab sticking out at the left and tuck into pocket.

12. Bend top ("stone") end and bottom end toward each other, forming a loop.

 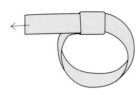 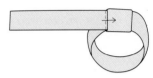

13. Insert bottom end under top layer of stone. Slide through until it comes out the other side of the stone.

14. Pull loose end to adjust size of Ring. Try on your finger to test.

15. When ring band fits your finger, set the size by folding the loose strip over the stone.

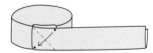 

16. Fold strip diagonally down so top edge lies over folded edge at left.

17. Bend strip back and slip up through ring. Crease strip at bottom edge of ring band.

18. Fold end of strip down so that height of strip will equal height of stone.

Note: If you made the size of your ring band very small, part of the overhang you folded down in step 18 may lie over stone. If this is the case, cut off the part that lies over stone.

19. Fold strip down over stone, then tuck into triangular pocket.

20. Finished Ring.

For Secret Ring: Slip tab back out of triangular pocket. Insert a tiny photo or secret message and tuck tab back into pocket. The tab will keep your secret hidden.

DIAMOND RING
by Ranana Benjamin

◆ ◆ ◆ ◆

Fold Secret Ring up to step 15.

1. Fold strip diagonally down so that top edge lies over folded edge at left. Unfold.

2. Repeat last step, this time bringing bottom edge of strip diagonally up to lie on left folded edge. Unfold.

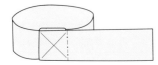

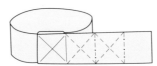

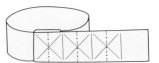

3. The two creases you just made form an X at left end of your strip. Mountain-fold strip back at right end of X. Crease and unfold.

4. You now have an X enclosed in a square at left side of your strip. Repeat steps 1 through 3 two more times, creating two more X patterns in squares on your strip.

5. Put a vertical mountain fold through center of each X. After each crease is made, unfold and make next crease.

Check your model. All diagonal creases should be valley folds, all vertical creases should be mountain folds.

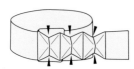

6. Starting at first X, push in at vertical mountain fold that divides X in half. Using existing creases, collapse small square that outlines X into a half-closed waterbomb base form. Repeat on next two X patterns.

7. Tuck tab at end of strip into pocket on ring band. (If tab is too long and extends out other end, you can cut off a little to shorten tab before inserting.)

8. Finished ring. **Side view**

TEARDROP ORNAMENT
by Rae Cooker

◆ ◆ ◆

Paper: Origami paper, foil paper, wrapping paper, or decorated handmade Japanese papers.
For the ornament, you'll need a 4″ to 6″ (10 to 15 cm) square.
For earrings, you'll need approximately 2″ (5 cm) square.

The side flaps will now be locked together in pairs at the base of your model. You will have four double flaps—two double flaps on the right and two double flaps on the left.

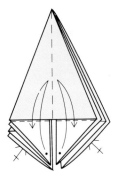

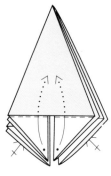

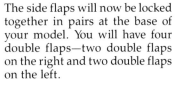

Follow the instructions for the umbrella base through step 6 to get to a squashed preliminary base.

1. Below the tall triangle are four small triangle "feet"—two in front and two in back. Lift both front triangle feet as far up as they will go. Unfold. Turn over and repeat behind.

2. Hold model loosely. Using the crease you just made, tuck each small triangle underneath raw edge of tall triangle. Repeat behind.

3. Begin to lift up one double flap as if you were turning the page of a book, but stop when the flap is standing straight up, at a right angle to the rest of the model.

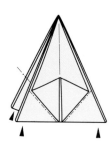

4. Insert finger between double layers. At the same time push up at bottom edge where layers are locked together until entire flap squashes flat.

5. Squash fold: Repeat steps 3 and 4 on remaining three double flaps.

6. Insert finger into pocket formed by squash fold and open out slightly. Repeat on other three pockets.

7. Finished Teardrop Ornament. Hang from a thread or wire.

ORIGAMI EARRINGS

You will need:

Earring Clasp

Attachment

Thread or wire   **Wire post with looped end**   **Twisted wire with loop**

Small origami model

Teardrop ornament   **Inside-Outside Ornament** *by Molly Kahn* (Preliminary and waterbomb bases slipped one inside the other.)   Traditional Crane

Optional

Small Beads

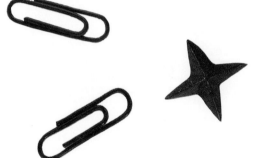

Depending on which model, clasp (finding), and attachment you choose, when assembling your earrings you may also need:

• needle for inserting thread
• adhesive
• small pliers
• wire cutter
• protective coating

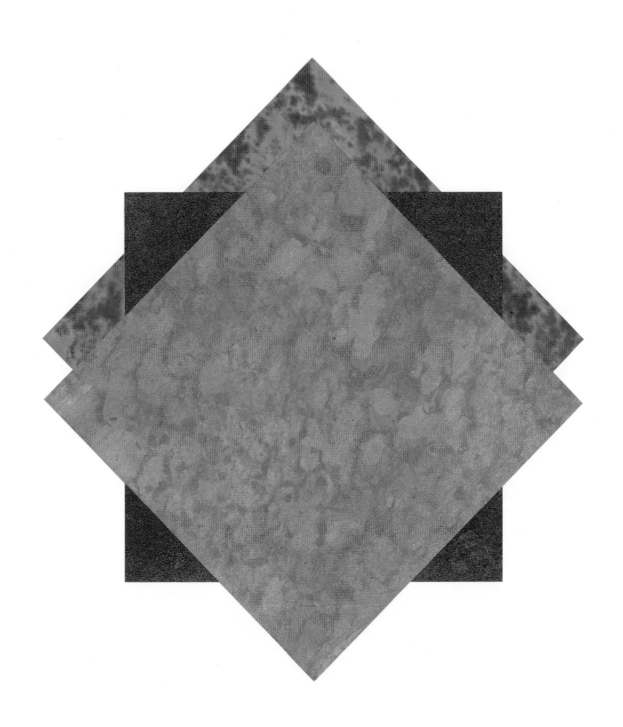

Part III

PAPERS
AND
SPECIAL
TECHNIQUES

WASHI PAPER

Washi paper is very high-quality paper made in Japan. Unlike most commercially available paper, it is not produced in huge quantities by machines, but is handmade in Japan using special techniques and materials. Some papers are left in a neutral color or given a solid color, but much washi paper is also made with exquisite designs and patterns, some so elegant they almost appear to be brocaded fabric. Because of the paper's softness, origami models made with washi will give a different effect than those made with most other papers. Washi paper is not as readily available as other kinds of paper and can be quite expensive, especially for the more decorative patterns. Nevertheless washi paper will add greatly to the strength and beauty of the finished model.

PACKAGED ORIGAMI PAPER

The most common packaged origami paper you will find has a solid color on one side and is white on the reverse side. Most packages contain a rainbow of colors; occasionally you may find packages containing only one color. While these packaged papers commonly come in 6" inch (15 cm) squares, you can usually also find 3"-inch (7.5 cm), 4½"-inch (12 cm), and 10"-inch (25 cm) squares. As the popularity of origami has grown, so has the variety of packaged papers made for folding. Such paper is now available in an exciting assortment of patterns, designs, and textures. With such an array of papers, part of the folding process becomes deciding which pattern or color will look best with which model.

FOIL PAPER

Foil paper is not the aluminum foil used in the kitchen. Such foil is too thin to fold successfully unless you bond it first to another paper. (See page 66.) Foil paper suitable for origami is manufactured with a layer of foil bonded to a layer of paper. The foil side may be smooth or have an embossed pattern. It is readily available in rolls along with other gift wraps, especially in gold, silver, green, and red at Christmastime. It is also available for sale as precut squares along with other packaged origami papers.

The brilliant, shiny surface of foil paper can be very attractive for certain models, while others may look better with a more subdued surface. Foil offers the advantage of allowing you to shape and mold the paper. One disadvantage, however, is that crease lines are usually more obvious on foil paper, so if your model requires a lot of precreasing, you may end up with several unwanted crease lines showing on the finished model.

WRAPPING PAPER

Most wrapping papers are ideal for origami. Choose a weight and pattern suitable for the model you are making. Paper used by florists to wrap flowers can also be suitable for origami. One type of paper to avoid, however, is heavyweight, highly glossed wrapping paper. This paper tends to crack along a crease line and creases do not stay well, so a finished model will tend to unfold.

WALLPAPER

The key word here is *paper*. Many wall coverings today are made from vinyl, which will not fold well. If "all-paper" wallpaper cannot be found, look for wallpaper that has a paper backing. Among the wallpapers made from paper, some may crack excessively when folded, but others will fold well, and when used for an appropriate model can yield some spectacular results.

FREE PAPER

One of the appeals of origami is its low cost and the minimal amount of materials required. Indeed, there are many excellent sources of papers that cost absolutely nothing. Just bear in mind that different weights and types of paper should be matched to the appropriate kind of model. (Most origami models require a lightweight paper.) Here is a list of some "free" sources of paper; keep your eyes open and you will probably discover others.

- discarded flyers
- used envelopes from greeting cards
- foil linings from envelopes
- business envelopes with an interesting pattern on the inside
- leftover wallpaper
- leftover gift wrap
- sample books of wallpaper
- leftover florist paper

- paper bags
- decorative shopping bags
- old magazine covers
- decorative photos or drawings from last year's calendar
- old business cards
- computer paper
- stationery
- maps

PAPER PAINTING

Materials:

- old newspaper to protect work surface
- sponges
- liquid watercolors (come in dropper bottles, available at art-supply stores)
- cup of water
- paper sturdy enough to withstand slight dampening (suggested: paper side of foil-backed paper, kraft paper, paper bag paper, stationery, onion skin paper)
- wooden spring clothespins (optional)

(Note: Besides liquid watercolors, you can experiment with other types of paint, such as acrylic paint thinned with water, for example.)

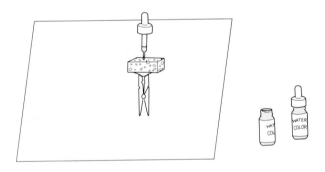

1. Cover table or other work surface with several layers of newspaper or other protective covering.

2. Place over newspaper the paper you wish to paint.

3. Cut sponge into smaller pieces. Simple rectangles (approximately 2" x 1½" is a convenient size) will work or you can cut the sponge into patterns or shapes. A pattern or waffling on the surface of your sponge can be useful in creating interesting patterns on your paper.

4. Dampen sponge by dipping it in water, then squeeze all the water out.

5. Clamp the clothespin to one end of the sponge. (If you don't mind getting watercolor on your hands, you can hold the sponge directly.)

6. Pick a color and drop a few drops on the end of the sponge.

7. Using the clothespin as a handle, dab the paper with the end of the sponge on which you put color. If too much color comes out of the sponge, dab it onto a piece of scrap paper first until the dye comes out in an amount that will color your paper without soaking it.

8. Experiment with these different methods of painting your paper:

- After you have added one color to your paper, change sponges and add another color.

- To lighten the color or create a bleeding effect with colors running into one another, slightly dampen your paper with a moist sponge before adding color.

- If you want your paper to be a solid color, slide your sponge across the paper in long strokes instead of dabbing. Use horizontal and then vertical strokes to avoid a streaked look. If the sponge does not go across paper easily, you may want to dampen the paper a little first.

- Instead of using a different sponge for each color, you can achieve another interesting effect by dropping two or three colors on the end of one sponge. Try to separate the colors slightly or they will end up blending, and instead of two or three separate colors you will have a new color. You can now create multicolored swirls, stripes, or spots with one touch of your sponge.

- You may want to give your paper a background color. If so, let it dry, and then add a pattern.

- Experiment with other ways of transferring the color onto the paper, such as placing the color on a piece of string and dragging it over or dabbing it on the paper.

DUO PAPER

In some origami models, both sides of the paper may show on the finished model. If your paper is white on the reverse side and you prefer the effect of two contrasting colors or a color and a pattern, you may be able to find wrapping paper or special origami paper, called duo paper, that has a different color on each side. In addition, you can achieve some very dramatic results, by trying one of these methods:

- Use the paper-painting techniques on this page to give a color or pattern to one side of your paper.

- Start with, or cut, two sheets into squares of the same size. Place the sheets together, with their back or white sides facing each other. Treat this double layer of paper as one sheet and fold the model as usual.

- Use a spray adhesive such as Spray Mount™ (available in art-supply stores) to join your two sheets together before folding. When using a spray adhesive, be sure you are in a well-ventilated space, or outdoors. Protect the area where you will be working with lots of old newspaper. Place the smaller of the two papers you wish to bond together on top of newspaper with the back side up. Spray the sheet with adhesive. Carefully lift this sheet and lay it over the second sheet, back sides touching. Press flat. Use a scissors or paper cutter to cut the bonded papers to the size and shape you need for your model.

- Remember that it is always the back side of each sheet that is bonded to the other.

Here are some combinations you can try:

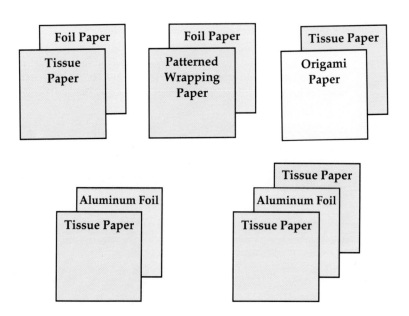

COPIER-DESIGNED PAPERS

You can use a photocopying machine to create interesting patterns on paper. Look through books, advertisements, wrapping papers, and decorated bags for geometrics and other patterns to photocopy, then use one of the following methods to copy the pattern onto white or colored photocopier paper:

- Copy the design as is.

- Enlarge or reduce the design.

- Move paper on the glass as the photocopier is operating to give a swirling effect.

- Experiment with photocopying textured surfaces such as a crumpled sheet of aluminum foil.

WET FOLDING

Some heavy papers that are not ordinarily ideal for folding are excellent candidates for wet folding. The water softens the paper so it does not crack when folded, and because of the stiffness of the paper, your model, when dry, will be much sturdier than if folded from softer paper. A wet-folded model also offers the folder the option of shaping a model such as an animal into a more three-dimensional form, giving it a more sculptured, lifelike appearance.

The technique of wet folding was pioneered by the Japanese origami master, Akira Yoshizawa.

Technique:

The main idea is to keep the paper *slightly* damp while you are folding. If you are using paper that will crack if not wet, dampen it before doing any folding. If you are using stiff paper that you want to be able to mold later, it is preferable to do some of the beginning folds first (such as a preliminary or waterbomb base), and then begin dampening the paper.

Fill a shallow bowl with some water. Dampen a sponge or washcloth in the water and use it to gently moisten your paper. Be careful not to wet the paper too much, especially at points on the paper where you will have a lot of intersecting creases. An example is the very center of the paper, which will tend to weaken from the many creases there and will tear if too wet.

As you continue folding, the paper will have a tendency to dry. Keep using your sponge or washcloth to dampen areas you are working on that have dried.

When the model is completely folded you can begin to mold and shape the paper to give the animal more form. If the paper is not damp enough to allow shaping, use your sponge to dampen it, or at this point you can spray your model lightly with a spray bottle or water mister. If necessary, paper towels can be used to stuff inside the model. Specific positions of joints or other features can be held in place until the model dries by wrapping them with wire or holding with clips. These (including the paper-towel stuffing) are all removed when the paper is dry. The finished model will not only be more three-dimensional, but will be very sturdy and retain its sculpted shape.

CUTTING A SQUARE FROM A RECTANGLE

Method #1

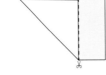

Cut along the raw edge, then unfold the diagonal fold.

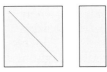

The leftover rectangular strip can be used for making smaller squares.

Method #2
(For a square without a diagonal crease.)

Position two rectangular sheets of identical size as shown. Cut the bottom sheet along the raw edge of the top sheet.

The undersheet is now square. If you need a second square, turn both layers over and cut the larger sheet using the raw edge of the square as your guide.

CUTTING A SQUARE FROM AN IRREGULARLY SHAPED PIECE OF PAPER

1. To get a straight edge: Make a fold near one end, fairly close to the edge of paper. Unfold and cut on the crease you just made.

2. Fold the straight edge on itself (point A will lie over point B). Crease and unfold. Cut on the crease you just made.

3. You now have two straight edges joined by a right angle. Fold the side straight edge up to the top edge.

4. Determine the size you would like your square to be and mark this amount at the top double raw edge. Beginning the fold at this mark, bring the point down to lie on the folded edge.

5. Cut along the raw edge and open out to find a square.

ADHESIVES

While paperfolders generally try to avoid the use of adhesives, models to be used for display (such as the Cactus Plant) or worn as jewelry may need the added security of a little glue when assembling. Here are some gluing tips to keep in mind:

- A white glue can generally be used when gluing paper to paper.

- When attaching something to foil paper or metal (such as a wire post or pin clasp), use Duco Cement™. When using this cement on a model folded of foil paper, try not to use any on an exposed surface of the model, since it may remove the foil coating or color from the paper and spoil your model.

- Only a very small amount of adhesive is generally needed. Squeeze a little onto a scrap piece of cardboard and use a toothpick to apply.

- If possible, use a tiny clothespin or paper clip to hold the paper in place until the adhesive dries.

PROTECTING ORIGAMI MODELS

Depending on the intended use of your origami model, you may wish to add a protective coating to help preserve the model. This is especially true when using origami models as jewelry.

First experiment with a scrap of paper before coating your model, since some papers and foils may change color or become transparent from the coating medium. Check first to see if you like the new effect. Here are some methods you can try:

- Krylon™ clear acrylic spray. This offers the lightest form of protection and will change the look and feel of your model the least. This spray is also useful for preventing the colors on paper you have hand-painted from bleeding if it should accidentally get wet. This spray is available in hardware, paint, or art-supply stores. Use the spray outdoors or in a well-ventilated area and spray into a box or space covered with newspaper. Paper can be sprayed either before or after it is folded.

- Clear nail polish. Coat your model using the brush provided in the jar. Some clear nail polishes may yellow with time.

- Joli Glaze™. A liquid plastic medium in a can that is sold in craft-supply stores and is a more permanent form of protection. Your model should be attached to a wire or thread so it can be dipped into can and then hung to dry for several hours. This preservation method will give the model a glazed look; it may also cause the color to lighten, turn transparent, or bleed.

- Sculpey Glaze™. This has the advantage of being water soluble. You can paint it on with a brush or thin it with water in a container so that the model can be dipped. It is sold in craft and art-supply stores. Because this glaze is water soluble, it may cause the colors on hand-painted papers to bleed.

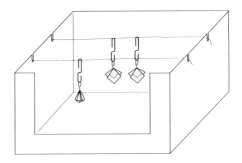

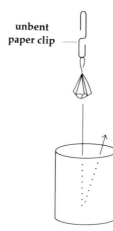

unbent
paper clip

The Friends of the Origami Center of America offers a complete selection of origami books as well as a wide variety of packaged origami papers. Their selection comes from the United States, Japan, England, and Italy. All books and paper must be ordered by mail. For a source list, send a self-addressed envelope with two first-class stamps to:

The Friends of the Origami Center of America
15 West 77th Street
New York, NY 10024-5192

STORES

Japanese bookstores and gift shops frequently carry packaged origami paper. Japanese food stores may also carry this paper.

Greeting card stores carry a variety of gift wrap.

Some art-supply stores may carry washi paper, marbleized paper, or packaged origami paper.

Here is a list of some stores and the papers they carry:

P—Packaged origami paper
B—Origami books
M—Marbleized paper
W—Washi paper
C—Catalog or sample book available, call or write for information

U.S.A.

Chicago
Aiko's Art Materials Import, Inc.
3347 North Clark Street
Chicago, Illinois 60657
(312) 404-5600
   P, B, M, W, C

Paper Source
730 North Franklin, Suite 111
Chicago, Illinois 60610
(312) 337-0798
   M, W, C

Denver
Kobun-Sha
1255 19th Street
Denver, Colorado 80202
(303) 295-1845
   P, B

Los Angeles
Bunkado
340 East First Street
Los Angeles, California 90012
(213) 625-8673
   P, B

New York City Area
Books Nippon
115 West 57th Street
New York, New York 10019
(212) 582-4622
   P, B

New York Central Art Supply
62 Third Avenue
New York, New York 10003
(212) 473-7705
(800) 950-6111 (outside NY)
   P, M, W, C

JAM Envelope and Paper Company
621 Sixth Avenue
New York, NY 10011
(212) 255-4593
   Stationery in a wide variety of colors, weights and textures

Kate's Paperie
8 West 13th Street
New York, NY 10011
(212) 633-0570
   M, W, C—also carries imported giftwrap

Yaohan Plaza
595 River Road
Edgewater, New Jersey 07020
(201) 941-9113
   Yaohan Foodstore—P
   Kinokuniya Bookstore—B

Zen Oriental Bookstore—Tokyo Shoten
521 Fifth Avenue
New York, NY 10175
(212) 697-0840
   P, B

Orlando (EPCOT Center)
Mitsukoshi
Japan Pavilion—EPCOT Center
P.O. Box 10000
Lake Buena Vista, Florida 32830
(407) 827-8513
   P, B

San Francisco
The Paper Tree
1743 Buchanan Mall
San Francisco, California 94115
(415) 921-7100
   P, B, W

Seattle
Uwajimaya
6th South & South King
Seattle, Washington 98104
(206) 624-6248
   P, B

Canada

Toronto
The Japanese Paper Place
966 Queen Street West
Toronto, Ontario M6J 1G8
Canada
(416) 533-6862
   P, B, M, W

The increasing popularity and international appeal of origami is evidenced today in the number of organizations around the world devoted to origami. Origami societies usually publish a regular newsletter or magazine with news of interest to paperfolders and diagrams for new models. They also hold regular meetings and yearly conventions which may include classes and displays of new creations. National organizations currently exist in:

Argentina   Mexico
Australia   New Zealand
Belgium   Peru
England   Poland
France   Singapore
Germany   Soviet Union
Holland   Spain
Italy   United States
Japan

In North America, regional origami clubs hold meetings in:

California   Michigan
Colorado   New Jersey
Florida   New York
Georgia   Ohio
Illinois   Ontario
Kentucky   Oregon
Manitoba   Pennsylvania
Maryland   Texas
Massachusetts

For information on any of these national and regional origami groups or information on origami in general contact:

The Friends of the Origami Center of America
15 West 77th Street
New York, NY 10024–5192

British Origami Society
253 Park Lane
Poyton, Stockport
Cheshire, SK12 IRH
England

Note: Numbers in italics refer to models with instructions.